Welcome

TO DINOCORN WORLD!

Thank you for choosing my coloring book. I hope you will enjoy it. Let me know if you like it and leave a rating in the review section on Amazon. This will help me create and improve more products.

Color testing page

Look so nice...

So cute...

Pretty like me!

Girly things

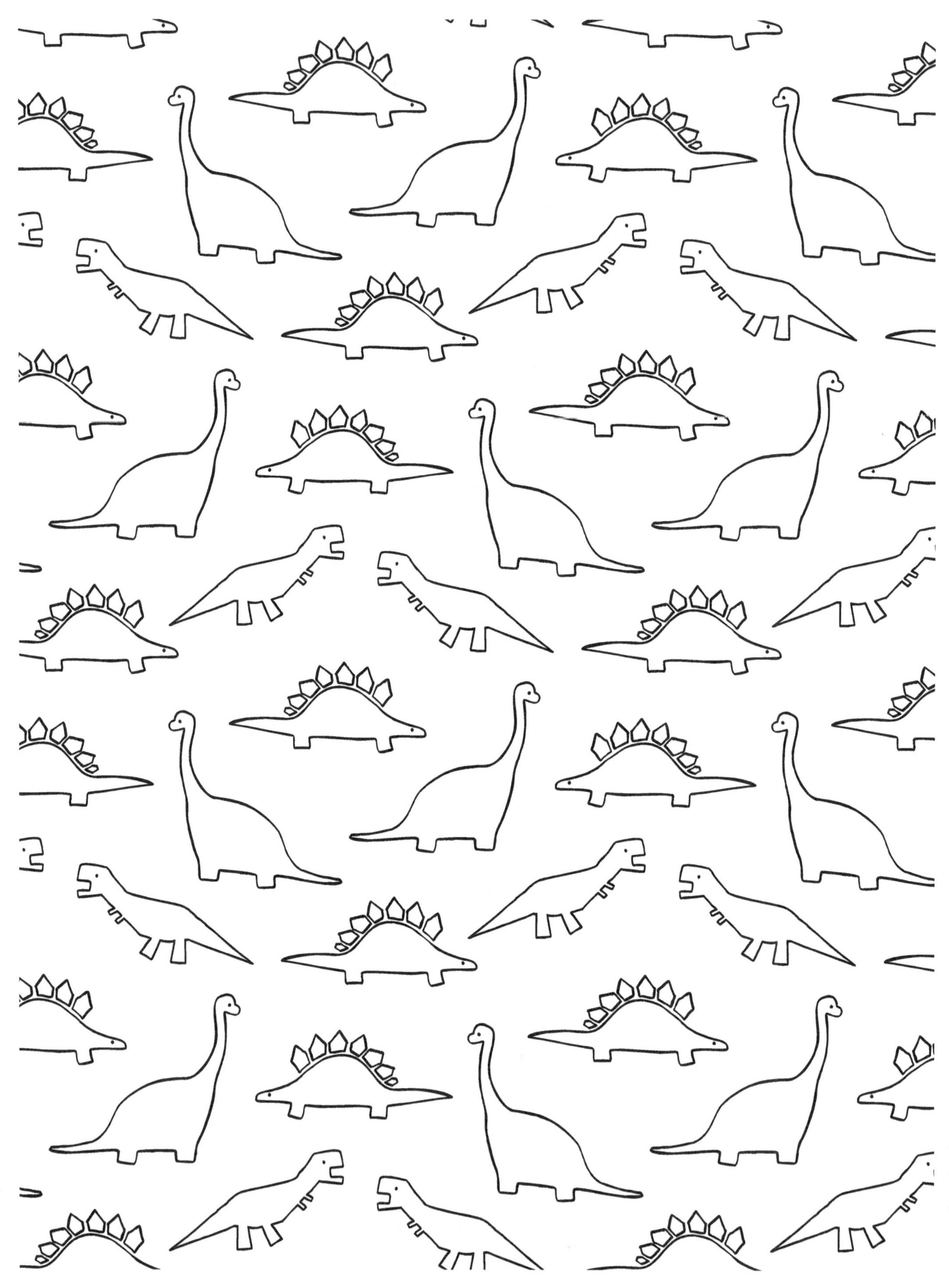

Cute DinoWorld

Little Dinocorn

Cute everywhere

Dinocorn friends

French style, baby

What a beautiful
Dinoworld!

Enjoy little things

Dinocorn

Big little princess

Shopping time!

I hate Mondays

Bridecorn to be

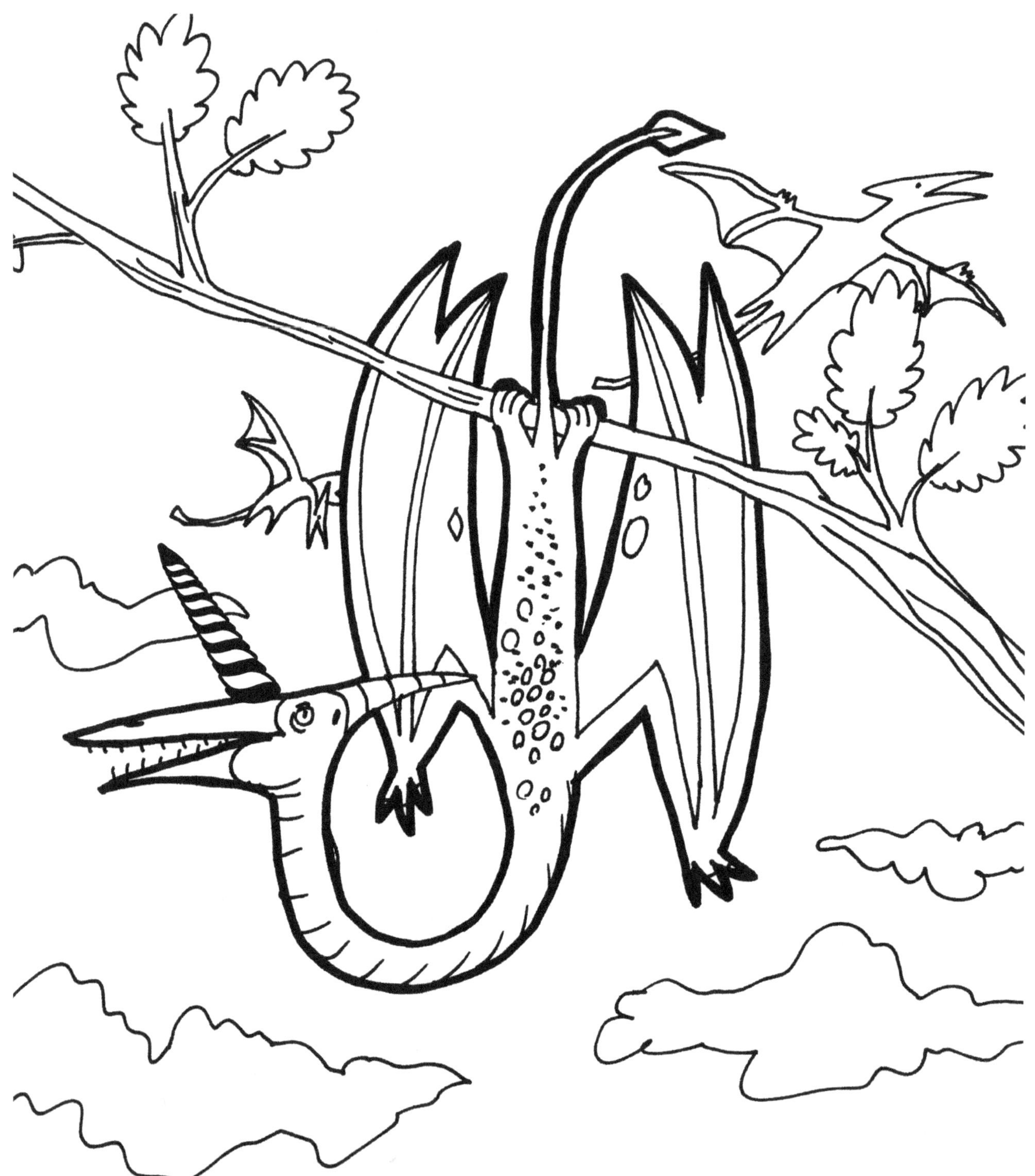

Little nap never killed nobody

Do not argue with me!

Dinocorn planet

How do I look!

Little Friends

Time for some food!

Cute Dinobear

Sweet as always

You can be sad sometimes

I'm coming to you

Underwater dinocorn

There is only one queen

Little princess

It's a good day

Beautiful Dinoworld

Will you marry me?

Pretty little girl

ILLUSTRATIONS:

Canva

Creative fabrica

Vecteezy